The Mini Mandala Coloring Book

Susanne F. Fincher

Shambhala
Boston & London
2014

Shambhala Publications, Inc.
Horticultural Hall
300 Massachusetts Avenue
Boston, Massachusetts 02115
www.shambhala.com

This book is a slightly revised edition of *Coloring Mandalas 1* (Shambhala, 2000).

9 8 7 6 5 4 3 2

Printed in the United States of America

♾ This edition is printed on acid-free paper that meets the American National Standards Institute Z39.48 Standard.
♻ This book is printed on 30% postconsumer recycled paper.
For more information please visit www.shambhala.com.
Distributed in the United States by Penguin Random House LLC
and in Canada by Random House of Canada Ltd

Designed by James D. Skatges

ISBN 978-1-61180-176-7

Introduction

The word *mandala* is Sanskrit for "sacred circle" or "cycle." The oldest mandalas are rock carvings found at Neolithic sites, where they represent the sun, moon, and seasons. Perhaps creating these images helped our ancestors make sense of the world and their place in it. Interestingly, similar mandala designs naturally appear in the drawings of today's young children as they are discovering

Children's mandalas (top row) resemble ancient rock carvings (bottom row).

themselves. These youngsters may well be repeating the same steps from cognition to self-awareness taken by our ancestors long ago.

In religious traditions of the East, mandalas are embedded in many activities even to this day. Mandalas are created to prepare a space for religious rituals. It is believed that creating and meditating on mandalas helps individuals invoke desirable states of consciousness and anchors spiritual seekers on the desired path toward enlightenment. Continuing an ancient custom, South Indian village housewives create mandalas each morning by sprinkling rice flour on their clean-swept front stoops in hopes of inviting positive energies into their households.

Christian rose windows are light-filled mandalas that inspire an experience of the divine.

Mandalas have a rich history in European traditions as well. Medieval European churches are filled with mandalas: labyrinth floor mosaics, domed ceilings, and dazzling stained-glass rose windows. In Europe, however, the importance of the circle in spiritual practice waned with the shift toward scientific inquiry.

JUNG AND THE MANDALA

We owe the reintroduction of mandalas into Western thought to C. G. Jung, the Swiss psychoanalyst. In his pioneering exploration of the unconscious through his own art making, Jung observed the motif of the circle spontaneously appearing. The circle drawings reflected his inner state at that moment. Familiarity with the philosophical writings of India prompted him to adopt the word *mandala* to describe these circle drawings he and his patients made.

Jung recognized that the urge to make mandalas emerges during moments of intense personal growth. Their appearance indicates that a profound rebalancing process is underway in the psyche. The result of the process is a more complex and better-integrated personality. As Jungian analyst Marie-Louise von Franz explains,

The mandala serves a conservative purpose—namely, to restore a previously existing order. But it also serves the creative purpose of giving

5

expression and form to something that does not yet exist, something new and unique. . . . The process is that of the ascending spiral, which grows upward while simultaneously returning again and again to the same point. (Cited in Jung 1964, 225)

Creating mandalas helps stabilize, integrate, and reorder inner life.

ARCHETYPAL STAGES OF THE GREAT ROUND OF MANDALA

In the 1970s American art therapist Joan Kellogg developed ideas about mandalas and personal growth. She called her theory "Archetypal Stages of the Great Round of Mandala" (or "the Great Round"). Kellogg identified mandala designs associated with twelve stages in a complete cycle of growth related to the flux and flow of human experience. According to Kellogg, stages are visited again and again. Visits to some stages are preparation for life stages yet to come. Each visit offers an opportunity for deeper understanding, self-realization, and wholeness.

The Great Round can be applied to all human endeavors. Even activities like baking a pie have stages from beginning to end, as does the Great Round. For example, a pie maker might begin her baking when she has a vague dream of something delicious. When she awakens, she begins systematic steps such as learning how her mother cooks, practicing cooking on her own, and developing baking skills so that she can create the pie crust and filling. Then she surrenders her unbaked pie to the oven, and if all goes well, she removes a fragrant, mouthwatering pie: success! But the process does not stop there. Next the pie must be cut up and eaten. Soon it is completely consumed, leaving behind only the glow of satisfaction for the pie maker as she reflects on all the steps she has taken. The pie maker is then ready to fall asleep and dream another dream to bring into reality.

The stages of the Great Round can also be aligned with a lifetime: conception (stage 1); birth through childhood (stages 2–5); adolescence (stage 6);

Archetypal Stages of the Great Round of Mandala
(Kellogg 1978; drawn by Susanne Fincher 2003)

adulthood (stages 7–9); and aging, death or near death, and beyond (stages 10–12). This mandala coloring book includes mandalas from the twelve stages arranged in order from stage 1 to stage 12.

Stage 1 mandalas are dark, with little form other than the encircling circle. During this stage you may feel like a sleepwalker—drowsy and hardly aware of your surroundings.

Stage 2 mandalas are filled with soft light and are teeming with myriad undefined possibilities. During this stage you may experience feelings like the ones you had in infancy: lightness, bliss, and unquestioning loyalty.

Stage 3 mandalas are filled with spiraling lines. You may feel energized and excited about new, as yet undefined possibilities during this stage.

Stage 4 mandalas have a single prominent center symbol. This stage invites you to nurture something new: a project, a young creature, or a discovery about yourself.

Stage 5 mandalas have several circles around a center point. You are gathering your personal power during this stage.

Stage 6 mandalas are divided in half, with a center form emerging from the divide. When living this stage you experience conflicts that help you define who you are.

Stage 7 mandalas are circles often containing squares or crosses. During this stage you feel powerful, motivated, and clearheaded.

Stage 8 mandalas contain five-pointed stars, flowers, or lines rotating around a center. When in this stage, your energy turns outward toward practical matters that help you accomplish your goals.

Stage 9 mandalas are intricate, harmonious designs that convey a sense of serenity. You are reaping the rewards of your efforts and activities during this stage.

Stage 10 mandalas suggest the beginning of the end of this growth cycle through downward-pointing forms, gateways, and setting suns. You experience decreasing creative energy and productivity during this stage.

Stage 11 mandalas appear fragmented and disorderly, sometimes ugly—or strangely beautiful. You may feel anger, loss, or confusion as the familiar order of your life comes to an end during this stage.

Stage 12 mandalas incorporate uplifting motifs that may resemble birds ascending, fountains of light, or arms raised in awe. With this stage you can grasp the perfection of all you have experienced during the cycle of growth that's coming to an end and feel a sense of profound gratitude, joy, and renewal.

How to Use This Book

When you buy a mandala coloring book, you are responding to the same urge as mandala artists who feel compelled to create circular drawings. Here are just a few of the many rich opportunities that coloring mandalas offers.

Creativity: Mandalas for coloring provide a semi-structured art activity that is more comfortable than beginning with a blank piece of paper.

Health: Coloring mandalas exercises hand muscles and promotes hand-eye coordination.

Relaxation: The activity of coloring engages attention and stimulates rhythmic body movement. Coloring is something like meditation in that it gives your mind a focus and can help decrease racing thoughts.

Support: During challenging times, such as sitting at the hospital bedside of a sick friend, coloring mandalas can offer respite or a topic for conversation, or it can help you establish a personal space in unfamiliar surroundings.

Journaling: Mandalas can be colored and enjoyed during a multi-generational family weekend at the beach, a quiet day alone listening to music, or a gathering with friends for coffee and conversation. The completed mandalas become a visual reminder of the special times.

Group activity: Sharing copies of mandalas from this book and inviting members of a group to choose and color one can be a pleasant activity. Completed mandalas can be discussed in the group, exhibited, or used as a takeaway reminder of the group experience.

Color study: Picking colors can be a simple choice of favorites, an exploration of personal meanings attached to colors, or a cerebral exploration of color harmonies, depending on the intention of the artist at work on the mandala.

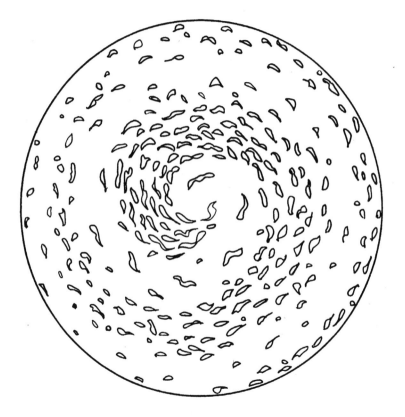

Mandala 11

As you experience stage 3, Labyrinth, you may feel that you have begun an important journey, though where your journey is leading you remains unknown. There is excitement, a sense of expectancy, and anticipation as the path opens before you.

Here is a way to decipher your color meanings through journaling: After completing your mandala, turn to your journal and list all the colors you see in your mandala. Beside each color, write word associations (whatever comes to mind). Read back through all you have written and summarize your personal meaning for each color.

Dreamwork: Color a mandala that reminds you of a dream you had the night before. This can be a good way to honor the dream, give the dream substance, or stimulate new insights about the meaning of the dream.

Self-knowledge: Learning about yourself from coloring mandalas can take many forms. Turning to a journal to write about your mandala is one of the best. Give your mandala a title. Then write about what the title suggests to you. Or, after using colors you like (or do not like), turn to your journal and write about why you like or dislike the colors. You might also try coloring with your nondominant hand, then writing about how working with less skillful muscle control was for you. Taking another approach, address your mandala as if it is a person, and finish statements such as "You are . . .," "You make me feel . . .," "I like (or don't like) . . .," or "You remind me of . . ." You might also let your mandala "respond" to your statements and write down what it has to tell you. These exercises can help you get to know the hidden parts of yourself that the mandala is bringing to your awareness.

More self-knowledge: Try choosing an appealing mandala to color from anywhere in the book, and then notice which stage of the Great Round the mandala is associated with. This may lead you to understand where you are on the Great Round at that moment. You can then better align your expectations with the energy you are experiencing. For example, if you choose a dreamy stage 2 mandala, do not expect yourself to be focused and highly productive that day. You may, however, be especially warm and nonjudgmental toward others.

Exploring the Great Round: This mandala coloring book offers several designs for each of the twelve stages in Joan Kellogg's Archetypal Stages of the Great Round of Mandala. Working in order through the book moves you through a complete cycle of the Great Round. This can be beneficial. Because you are usually more accustomed to some stages than others, coloring mandalas from less familiar stages may open you to living these stages more fully. As a result, you can come to appreciate and integrate formerly rejected or overlooked feelings and experiences.

For example, coloring mandalas from stages 1–5 may soothe your inner child. Coloring mandalas from stage 6 may give you an awareness of inner conflicts and the qualities that can bring them into harmony. Coloring mandalas from stages 7–8 may stimulate your productivity. Coloring mandalas from stages 9–10 may help you slow down and appreciate your accomplishments. Coloring mandalas from stages 11–12 may help you let go and open to a feeling of deep satisfaction about your life.

Remember: there is no right or wrong way to color a mandala. Enjoy!

REFERENCES

Boas, Franz. 1955. *Primitive Art*. New York: Dover Publications.

Gimbutas, Marija. 1991. *The Language of the Goddess*. San Francisco: Harper-SanFrancisco.

Jung, C. G. 1964. *Man and His Symbols*. Garden City, NY: Doubleday.

Jung, C. G. 1973. *Mandala Symbolism*. Princeton, NJ: Princeton University Press.

Kellogg, Joan. 2002. *Mandala: Path of Beauty* (3rd ed.). Belleaire, FL.: Association for Teachers of Mandala Assessment.

Mandalas for Coloring

Mandala 1

During stage 0, Clear Light, the profound simplicity of an empty circle invites, shelters, brings focus, and gives form. The empty circle suggests potential, defines a boundary, and establishes center and circumference. The circle is an image of God, of eternity, of union between the One and the many. It is the signature of the inner urge toward wholeness that Jung called the Self. Take a moment to ponder and discover what it means to you to enter the circle, to join this dance of the twelve stages of the Great Round and their mandala forms.

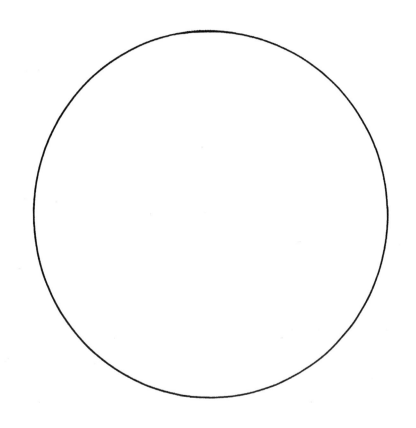

Mandala 2

During stage 1, Void, you experience a moment beyond ordinary clock time, a dreamtime when your inner world is profoundly reordered. In the metaphorical language of spirituality, it is a time when spirit enters matter and takes the form you know as your body.

Mandala 3

As spirit moves through matter, the rhythm of earthly existence is set in motion. Stage 1, Void, enfolds you in the pulsing web of life.

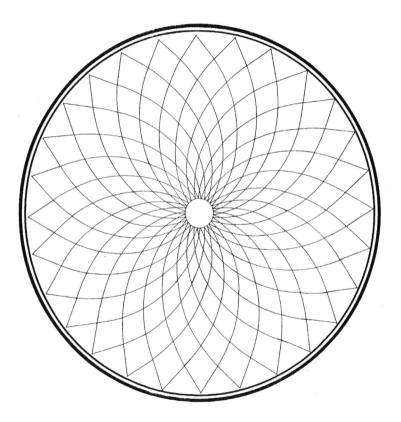

Mandala 4

During stage 1, Void, the consciousness that holds all possibilities and potential in seamless unity separates into the dualities familiar to you in your daily thoughts: yes/no, good/bad, I/not-I. Thus the One becomes the many.

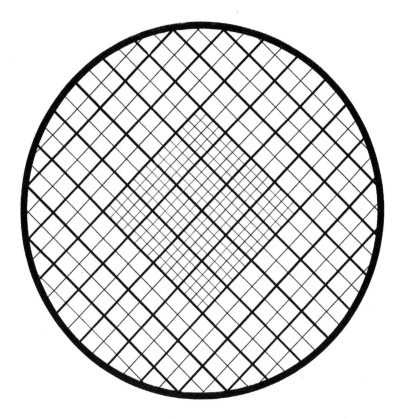

Mandala 5

Stage 2, Bliss, brings an experience of the boundless generativity of Life. This mandala of our Earth is a reminder that she is the womb supporting you as you are birthing yourself anew.

Mandala 6

Stage 2, Bliss, brings you the awareness that life is pregnant with possibilities. What brain-child will you choose to develop on this circling of the Great Round?

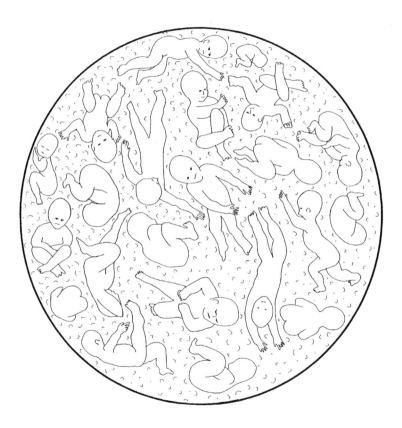

Mandala 7

The sky is filled with stars and your life is full of opportunities. You will be shaped by your choices. It is hard to focus on only one, but that is the challenge of stage 2, Bliss.

Mandala 8

Your experience of stage 2, Bliss, resonates with your earliest memories from birth or even before. The mystery of new life is celebrated in mandalas such as this one signifying the regenerative powers of the Mother Goddess, whom ancients worshipped as the source of life. (After an illustration in Marija Gimbutas, *The Language of the Goddess*)

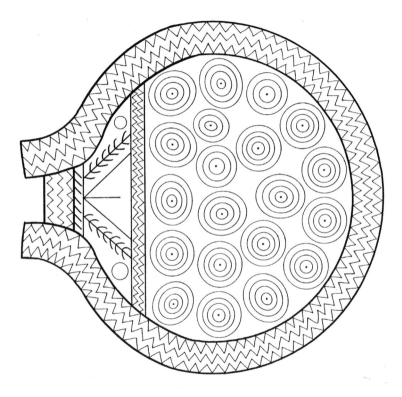

Mandala 9

Stage 3, Labyrinth, is a moment of engagement, of quickening, of seeing through to a new reality. Perhaps such moments inspired the medieval Irish monks who created designs such as this one. What appears to be a single endless meander is really two separate pathways crossing many times but never completely joining each other. Contemplative Christians see in this pattern the Trinity, God as three in one.

Mandala 10

Is it a shoal of fish? The spinning of the wind? Or a fetus nestling in its mother's womb? Spiraling motion suggests the movement from the Center as we spin ourselves into being during stage 3, Labyrinth.

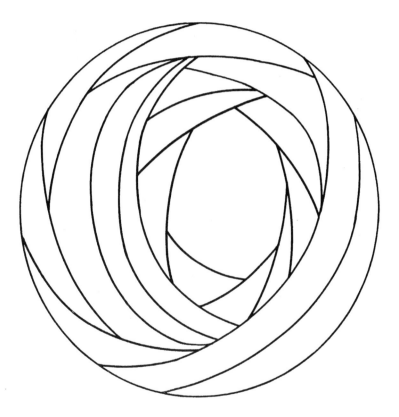

Mandala 12

Experiences of divergent realities, nonordinary states of consciousness, and extraordinary happenings occur during your time in stage 3, Labyrinth. Shamans cultivate their abilities to move in and out of this stage at will. Through it they access wisdom that can benefit their community. (After M. C. Escher)

Mandala 13

Stage 4, Beginning, is about cherishing the new, tenderly caring for your young inner self, or nurturing that brainchild singled out from the many available to you in stage 2, Bliss. It is as if you are pregnant with yourself. Treat yourself gently.

Mandala 14

During stage 4, Beginning, you are producing something new, even though its final form cannot yet be seen. This simple mandala design is found on the walls of a birthing chamber in an ancient palace on the island of Crete. Archeologists suggest that it may represent the cervix. You can use the dot as a beginning point for your own design. Perhaps it will reflect something you are "birthing." (After an illustration in Marija Gimbutas, *The Language of the Goddess*)

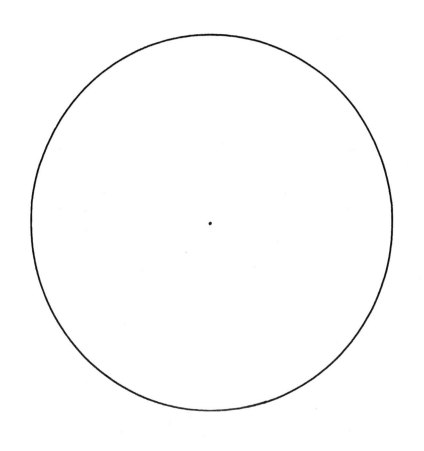

Mandala 15

Stage 4, Beginning, is a time when you hold close your tender new creation so that it can develop. Like the flower in this mandala, protectively enclosed in a circle, you contain and focus your energy when creating something new.

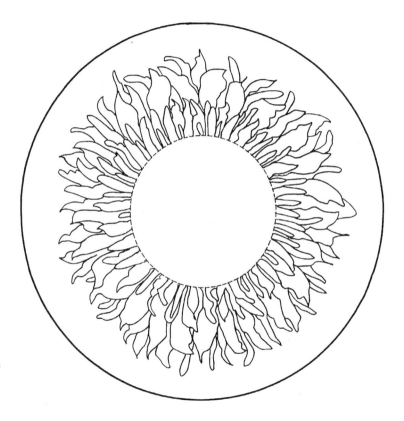

Mandala 16

During stage 4, Beginning, your energy can be used for growing ideas, for dreaming up creations, or for deepening your relationship with your inner self. As you focus your efforts on nurturing the new, you experience an intensification of heart energy, love of the sort that is unconditional and dedicated to serving others.

Mandala 17

During stage 5, Target, you experience a sense of urgency as you encounter limits that seem to block your progress. You may feel angry, scared, or confused. This mandala can be used to explore your feelings.

Inner circle: Name or draw those things that you fear most. Fill in the ring around the circle with a color that represents courage.

Second circle: Name or draw teachers, guides, and mentors, living or of the spirit world.

Third circle: Name or draw the negative thoughts and behaviors that arise from your fears.

Fourth circle: Name or draw positive behaviors that help you manage your fear.

Fifth circle: Write affirmations that address your fears. Read these aloud.

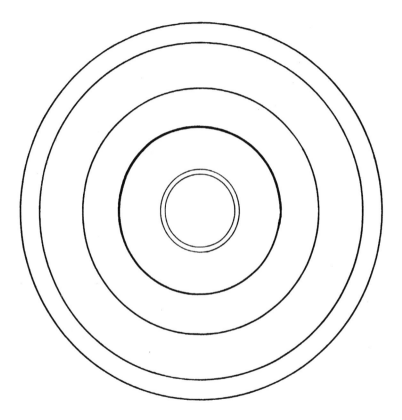

Mandala 18

During stage 5, Target, you may feel like a soldier patrolling your boundaries. Vigilance seems the only option when your perceptions make you feel as if you are the target of others' attacks—even when you are not. Mandalas here can sometimes look like wall after wall of protection and defense. Feeling safe is very important to you during this stage.

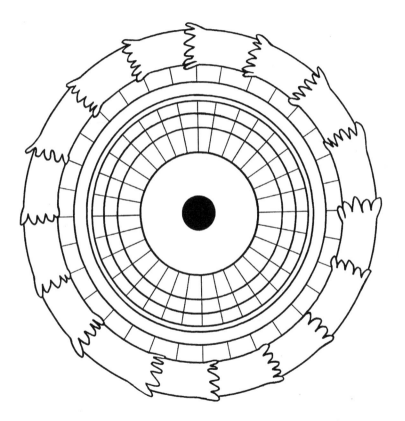

Mandala 19

Personal habits and other rituals help you feel safe during stage 5, Target, when emotions intensify. Like the strong walls of a castle sheltering a garden within, this Celtic mandala has mazelike bands of designs protecting tender leafy vines in the center.

Mandala 20

Circles within circles appear to be moving in opposite directions. Stage 5, Target, is about stirring your energy, like a race car revving its engine in preparation for the start of a race. (Inspired by a painted ceramic platter, Bulgaria, 4500–4300 B.C.E.)

Mandala 21

This mandala symbolizes an experience of inner conflicts, typical of stage 6, Dragon Fight. Do I love this or that? Shall I stay here or go there? When you can hold the tension of these opposites, rejecting neither option, for long enough, a third option appears that resolves the conflict. Notice the lines suggesting movement into the center of this mandala, the beginning of a new center point in the space between the opposite egg-like forms. Perhaps you will discover the resolution to some inner conflict as you color this mandala. (Based on a painted ceramic design, Ukraine, 3500 B.C.E.)

Mandala 22

Stage 6, Dragon Fight, is experienced during adolescence and other important transitions to a new phase in your life. Tribal peoples heighten the normal fear and stress of young people to intensify their initiation into adulthood. Initiates are given secret teachings about the animals that serve the tribe as helpers and guides to the spirit world. Such a special feeling for animals seems to have inspired the creation of the ancient pottery design on which this mandala is based. (After an illustration in Marija Gimbutas, *The Language of the Goddess*)

Mandala 23

When you endure the tension of the opposites during stage 6, Dragon Fight, a new viewpoint eventually emerges that transcends and resolves the conflict. So we see in this mandala the opposites of Mother Earth and Father Sky, male and female energy. The sun rising between the earth and sky signifies the new element appearing. Like the child that inherits qualities from both parents but is identical to neither, the solution to conflicts brings something entirely new to the situation.

Mandala 24

In stage 6, Dragon Fight, you come to a new understanding of yourself in relationship to your parents and what they taught you. This brings about the birth—or rebirth—of your ego, an occurrence that happens many times during your life. The "eye" at the center of this mandala signifies the ego, that part of you that you call "I."

Mandala 25

Stage 7, Squaring the Circle, brings your attention to thinking, learning, and discovering your unique talents and abilities. This mandala design was created during the Renaissance as an object of meditation. Committing it to memory was thought to draw up love, the life force in all things. (After Giordano Bruno)

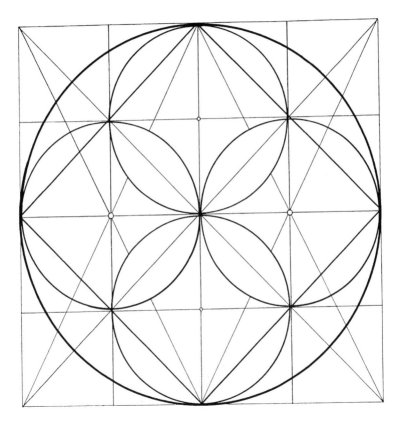

Mandala 26

During stage 7, Squaring the Circle, the resolution of inner conflicts creates a stronger, more complex personality. You may find yourself motivated by a sense of mission that engages your whole self in the accomplishment of worthy goals. This mandala, like a crusader's shield, boldly announces, "I am here."

Mandala 27

In stage 7, Squaring the Circle, feeling comfortable with yourself and your place in the scheme of things creates a firm foundation for identity. The harmonious balance between circles and squares seen in this mandala reflects the balancing of masculine and feminine energy you experience during this stage.

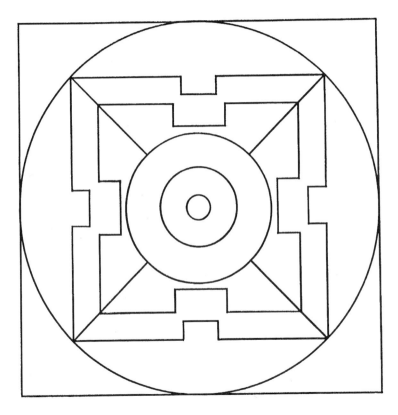

Mandala 28

During stage 7, Squaring the Circle, your ego—that which you call "I"—is aligned with your inner pattern of wholeness, the Self. Opening your connection with the Self, the true center of your psyche, frees energy for being, loving, and doing. Opposites that were in conflict have settled into a dynamic balance with each other, something like the pairs of wings in this mandala.

Mandala 29

With stage 8, Functioning Ego, you stand on your own two feet and reach out to engage the universe, like a flower turning its face to the sun. This is a time when inspirations are made reality through your own good efforts. You give your brainchild a form that can be seen and appreciated by others.

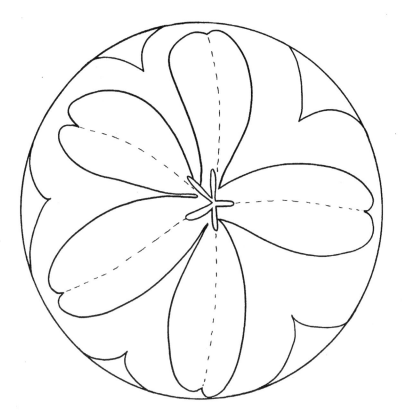

Mandala 30

During stage 8, Functioning Ego, your star rises as those around you take notice of your skills, abilities, and dedication. This five-pointed star mandala suggests a person standing firmly on both feet, arms outstretched, head held high. Such is the feeling of being in stage 8. (After a drawing by Deb Henderson)

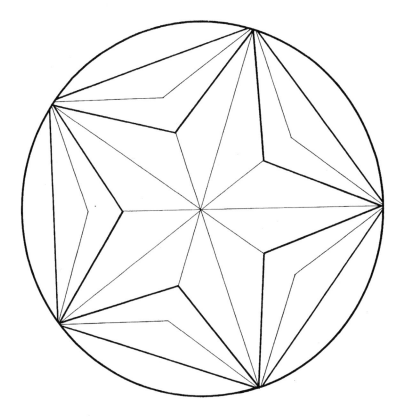

Mandala 31

During stage 8, Functioning Ego, you work comfortably within a group or alone as needed to accomplish your goals. You may amaze even yourself at all that is taking shape through your hands. In this Native American mandala, the static cross form sprouts wings and becomes a spinning swastika, ancient symbol of the sun. The movement in this design reflects the active doing that exemplifies this stage. (After an illustration in Franz Boas, *Primitive Art*)

Mandala 32

During stage 8, Functioning Ego, you reach out to touch, to take hold of life, to create new and wondrous things. Let your imagination give meaning to the five circles in this mandala. Do they represent the aspects of a complex project you are working on? Are they people with whom you seek to cooperate to accomplish your goals? Or are they reminders of the waxing phases of the moon and awareness of the need to work in harmony with the laws of nature?

Mandala 33

With stage 9, Crystallization, your work takes its final form. Surveying your labor of love, you find deep satisfaction in what you have accomplished. In this dynamic mandala, based on the number six, the interplay of lines brings one circle, then another, dancing into view. Just so, you review each facet of your creation and say to yourself, "This is good." (Based on a Hindu design signifying creation)

Mandala 34

A radiantly full flower suggests the essence of stage 9, Crystallization, a time when you experience understanding, satisfaction, and completion with a particular project or possibly a chapter in your life.

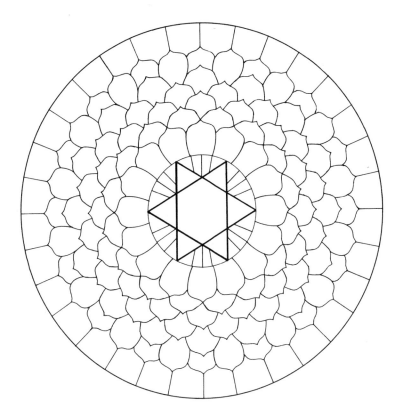

Mandala 35

Like a beautiful flower in full bloom, your intention for this turning of the Great Round is fulfilled in stage 9, Crystallization. This mandala recalls the rose windows in Gothic cathedrals, designed to pull your gaze again and again toward the center. Devout Christians use such windows to focus their attention on the Center, the Inner Christ.

Mandala 36

During stage 9, Crystallization, you begin to see through the appearances of things to grasp the fundamental structures of reality. This mandala is based on the Sri Yantra, a sacred Hindu design used for meditation. The single downward-pointing triangle in the center is a symbol of divine feminine energy, the source of all creation. Expanding outward from the center, upward- and downward-pointing triangles signify all male and female creatures coming into being. Lotus petals enclose the field of emanation, and lines that represent the four directions, the four elements, and other significant ordering principles border the whole. Because it is believed that the powers of the feminine are heightened during darkness, some practitioners recommend working with this yantra only during daylight hours.

Mandala 37

Stage 10, Gates of Death, marks the beginning of your disengagement from that which has held your attention for this circuit of the Great Round. This stage opens the equally important completion of the cycle that clears the way for a new beginning. You may feel compelled to turn your back on your accomplishments, to forgo security, or to let go of the way things have been, and to step through a gateway to a mysterious unknown. This commences a journey downward, into the depths of yourself.

Mandala 38

Stage 10, Gates of Death, brings you a sense of the relentless passage of time. The wheel of life turns on, sometimes up and sometimes down. Those caught up in their attachments try to hold back the sands of time. For others, willing to let go, all is as it should be.

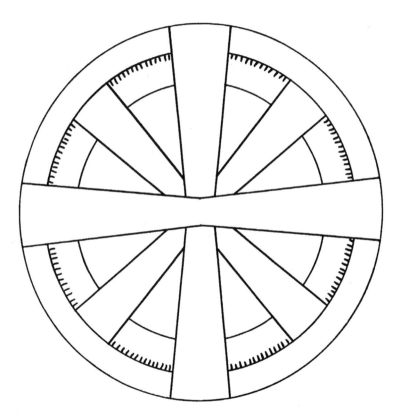

Mandala 39

Stage 10, Gates of Death, requires a sacrifice. The parting with what was can feel like a bittersweet pause at a crossroads, an urgent summons into alien territory, or even the ultimate surrender of crucifixion. You are being separated from that which is no longer needed. Celtic crosses like the one in this mandala dot the landscape of Scotland. Tall, silent, enduring stone, they stand against the sky washed by the winds and rains of countless seasons, reminders that even though things change, there is a part of you that lives on.

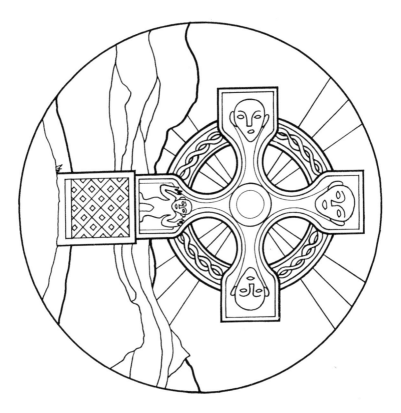

Mandala 40

During stage 10, Gates of Death, you may begin to see that destruction opens the way for creation. As in this mandala, based on the Kali Yantra of Hinduism, both energies are ever present. The eight-petaled lotus represents the goddess Kali in her nurturing maternal aspect. The inner circle, traditionally colored black, reveals her also as Destroyer, the dark womb that eventually absorbs all into nonbeing. And the center triangle, the ultimate symbol of divine feminine creative energy, holds the pearly spark of new life.

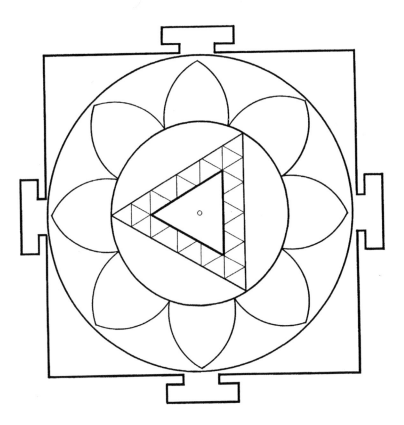

Mandala 41

During stage 11, Fragmentation, things come apart in your life. It is a time of increased confusion when you drop your groceries, the car won't start, your roof is leaking, and your power is cut off. It is the completion of the Great Round in a necessary period of chaos. Remember: to make an omelet, you must first break the eggs.

Mandala 42

During stage 11, Fragmentation, life seems shattered, with no hope of returning to the way it was before. Yet there are diamonds among the shards, if you can see them. Your challenge here is to let the chaos be and to remain calm and patient despite the turmoil. Have faith; the Great Round is ever turning, and this time does not last forever.

Mandala 43

During stage 11, Fragmentation, you feel lost, as if swallowed up in the belly of Jonah's whale. Like the killer whale depicted in this Native American design, you may feel your bones have been picked clean. All the better to become flexible, to learn to bend instead of breaking, to surrender to the shaping of spirit. (After an illustration in Franz Boas, *Primitive Art*)

Mandala 44

During stage 11, Fragmentation, you may dream of alien creatures, find yourself lost in the parking lot, or have puzzling encounters with familiar people. The disturbances are a natural part of releasing what is no longer needed, even when you think it is.

Mandala 45

During stage 12, Transcendent Ecstasy, you experience a shift from chaos to transformative wisdom, a reordering of all that was broken. This stage is a coming together of all that went before, a time of profound joy, when you feel perfectly in step with the cosmic dance. (After a drawing by Clara Klug)

Mandala 46

Arriving at stage 12, Transcendent Ecstasy, the last stage of the Great Round, you drink from the cup of wisdom. You grasp the pattern of your life in all its infinite beauty. Past and future merge into the eternal Now. Here, by the grace of God, not by willing or effort, you come to know the mystery of life.

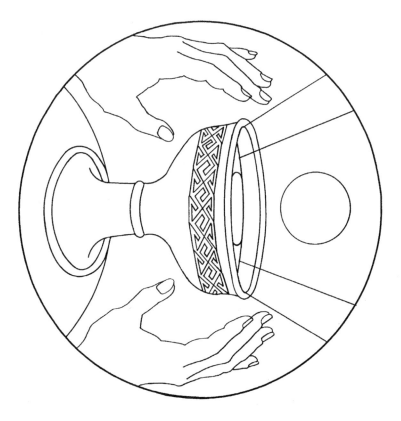

Mandala 47

Stage 12, Transcendent Ecstasy, is a moment of wholeness, of knowing rather than thinking. Mandalas such as this one signify the fruition of deep inner work through which you become aware that the true center of your psyche is the mysterious Self, that dynamic center Jung identified as an inner image of God. Pictured here is the lotus, a flowering plant that touches all four primal elements. Its roots are in the earth, its green growth is supported by water, its stalk ascends into the air, and its flower embraces the fiery sun. For Chinese mystics, the lotus is the mythic Golden Flower, symbol of the quest for enlightenment. (After an illustration in C. G. Jung, *Mandala Symbolism*)

Mandala 48

During stage 12, Transcendent Ecstasy, all is in perfect balance, a peaceful ending to the stages of change that are the Great Round. Be still and open yourself to knowing the true center of yourself, the One, and rest in the knowledge of who you are. Soon enough you will move on to the dreamtime, stage 1, Void, and a new beginning on the Great Round.

BOOKS BY SUSANNE F. FINCHER

Coloring Mandalas 1: For Insight, Healing, and Self-Expression

Coloring Mandalas 2: For Balance, Harmony, and Spiritual Well-Being

Coloring Mandalas 3: Circles of the Sacred Feminine

Coloring Mandalas 4: For Confidence, Energy, and Purpose

Creating Mandalas: For Insight, Healing, and Self-Expression

The Mandala Workbook: A Creative Guide for Self-Exploration, Balance,
and Well-Being